Cook Memorial Public Library

3 1122 01575 8381

JUL 29 2020

P9-CZV-275

20 FUN FACTS ABOUT THE EMPIRE STATE BUILDING

COOK MEMORIAL LIBRARY DISTRICT
413 N. MILWAUKEE AVE.
LIBERTYVILLE, ILLINOIS 60048

BY EMILY MAHONEY

Gareth Stevens
PUBLISHING

Please visit our website, www.garethstevens.com. For a free color catalog of all our high-quality books, call toll free 1-800-542-2595 or fax 1-877-542-2596.

Library of Congress Cataloging-in-Publication Data

Names: Mahoney, Emily Jankowski, author.
Title: 20 fun facts about the Empire State Building / Emily Mahoney.
Other titles: Twenty fun facts about the Empire State Building
Description: New York : Gareth Stevens Publishing, [2020] | Series: Fun fact file: world wonders | Includes index.
Identifiers: LCCN 2018039597| ISBN 9781538237663 (pbk.) | ISBN 9781538237687 (library bound) | ISBN 9781538237670 (6 pack)
Subjects: LCSH: Empire State Building (New York, N.Y.)–Juvenile literature. | New York (N.Y.)–Buildings, structures, etc.–Juvenile literature.
Classification: LCC F128.8.E46 M34 2019 | DDC 974.7/1–dc23
LC record available at https://lccn.loc.gov/2018039597

First Edition

Published in 2020 by
Gareth Stevens Publishing
111 East 14th Street, Suite 349
New York, NY 10003

Copyright © 2020 Gareth Stevens Publishing

Designer: Sarah Liddell
Editor: Kristen Nelson

Photo credits: Cover, p. 1 Matej Kastelic/Shutterstock.com; file folder used throughout David Smart/Shutterstock.com; binder clip used throughout luckyraccoon/Shutterstock.com; wood grain background used throughout ARENA Creative/Shutterstock.com; p. 5 cocozero/Shutterstock.com; p. 6 Scott Meivogel/Shutterstock.com; p. 7 GagliardiImages/Shutterstock.com; p. 8 aounphoto/Shutterstock.com; p. 9 Yiyi/Wikimedia Commons; p. 10 Lewis Hine/Durova/Wikimedia Commons; pp. 11, 12, 18 Bettmann/Contributor/Bettmann/Getty Images; p. 13 Lewis Hine/Svajcr/Wikimedia Commons; p. 14 Gage/Wikimedia Commons; p. 15 Al Gretz/Stringer/Archive Photos/Getty Images; p. 16 Hulton Archive/Stringer/Hulton Archive/Getty Images; p. 17 Movie Poster Image Art/Contributor/Moviepix/Getty Images; p. 19 STAN HONDA/Stringer/AFP/Getty Images; p. 20 William Anderson/Contributor/Getty Images News/Getty Images; p. 21 Brigitte Stelzer/Contributor/Hulton Archive/Getty Images; p. 22 dikobraziy/Shutterstock.com; p. 23 Vacclav/Shutterstock.com; p. 24 Dschwen/Wikimedia Commons; p. 25 Paper Cat/Shutterstock.com; p. 26 Bennett Raglin/Contributor/Getty Images Entertainment/Getty Images; p. 29 Mihai Simonia/Shutterstock.com.

All rights reserved. No part of this book may be reproduced in any form without permission in writing from the publisher, except by a reviewer.

Printed in the United States of America

CPSIA compliance information: Batch #CS19GS: For further information contact Gareth Stevens, New York, New York at 1-800-542-2595.

CONTENTS

Words in the glossary appear in **bold** type the first time they are used in the text.

SCRAPING THE SKY

There are many **skyscrapers** in New York City, but one stands out from the rest. Many people recognize the Empire State Building not only for its height, but also for its beauty.

The Empire State Building has an interesting history that many people may not know about, even though it's been in use since 1931. Read on to learn more about its construction, size, and use in one of the world's largest and busiest cities!

The Empire State Building is one of the tallest buildings in New York City. As of 2018, One World Trade Center was the tallest.

THE EMPIRE STATE BUILDING IS MORE THAN 200 TIMES TALLER THAN LEBRON JAMES!

The Empire State Building is 1,250 feet (381 m) tall. If you include the **antenna** at the top of the building, it's 1,454 feet (443.2 m) tall!

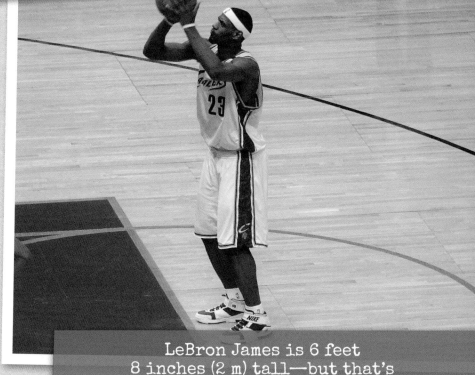

LeBron James is 6 feet 8 inches (2 m) tall—but that's still short compared to the Empire State Building!

THE EMPIRE STATE BUILDING HAS 102 FLOORS OPEN TO THE PUBLIC.

You can choose to take 1,872 stairs or one of the building's 73 elevators to the top. It may take a while to get to the top, but the view is amazing!

THE EMPIRE STATE BUILDING HELD THE OFFICIAL TITLE OF "WORLD'S TALLEST BUILDING" FOR ALMOST 40 YEARS.

No building on Earth was taller than the Empire State Building from 1931 to 1970. After that, the north tower of the original World Trade Center, also in New York City, became the tallest in the world for a short time.

Today, the Empire State Building is still easy to spot from most places in New York City since it's so tall!

SKYSCRAPERS AROUND THE WORLD

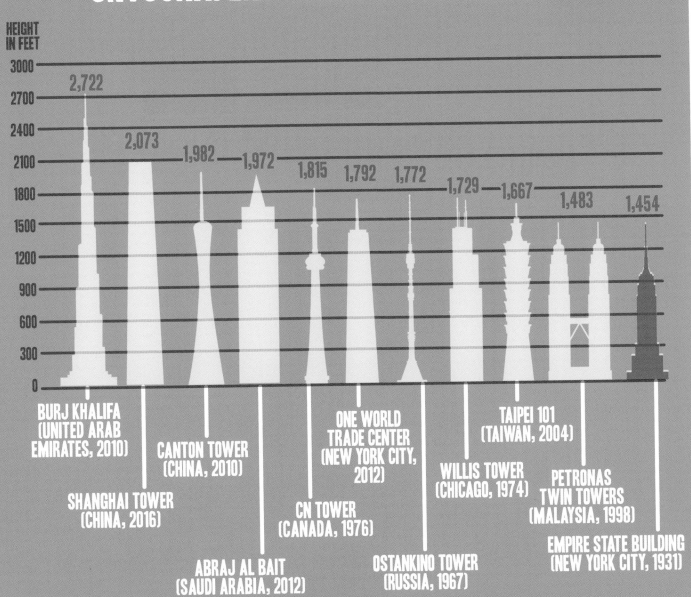

HEIGHT IN FEET

3000
2700
2400
2100
1800
1500
1200
900
600
300
0

2,722 — BURJ KHALIFA (UNITED ARAB EMIRATES, 2010)
2,073 — SHANGHAI TOWER (CHINA, 2016)
1,982 — CANTON TOWER (CHINA, 2010)
1,972 — ABRAJ AL BAIT (SAUDI ARABIA, 2012)
1,815 — CN TOWER (CANADA, 1976)
1,792 — ONE WORLD TRADE CENTER (NEW YORK CITY, 2012)
1,772 — OSTANKINO TOWER (RUSSIA, 1967)
1,729 — WILLIS TOWER (CHICAGO, 1974)
1,667 — TAIPEI 101 (TAIWAN, 2004)
1,483 — PETRONAS TWIN TOWERS (MALAYSIA, 1998)
1,454 — EMPIRE STATE BUILDING (NEW YORK CITY, 1931)

9

CONSTRUCTING A SKYSCRAPER

FUN FACT: 4

ABOUT 3,400 WORKERS HELPED TO BUILD THE EMPIRE STATE BUILDING.

Construction workers **labored** on Sundays and holidays to finish the job quickly. Official records show that five people died while working on the skyscraper.

The outside of the Empire State Building is made of limestone, granite, and brick.

IT TOOK ONLY 410 DAYS TO BUILD THE EMPIRE STATE BUILDING.

A year and 45 days was less time than construction of the large building was supposed to take. The steel work on the building also finished 12 days ahead of schedule, even though 60,000 tons (54,431 mt) of steel were used!

Imagine how fun it would have been to watch this building rising up so quickly!

ABOUT 4 1/2 STORIES OF THE BUILDING'S FRAME WERE BUILT EACH WEEK.

"Story" is another word for "floor." Stories are about 10 to 12 feet (3 to 3.7 m) tall. Today, inside this frame, there's 2.7 million square feet (250,838 sq m) of office space where people work!

THE EMPIRE STATE BUILDING HAD AN OFFICIAL PHOTOGRAPHER!

Hine's pictures can be found in a book called *Men at Work.*

Lewis Hine took pictures of the construction of the Empire State Building. He also photographed the men working on the skyscraper, whom he called "sky boys." At times, Hine was lifted more than 1,300 feet (396 m) in an open steel box to take pictures!

FUN FACT: 8

THE EMPIRE STATE BUILDING WAS FIRST LIT UP FROM WASHINGTON, DC!

On May 1, 1931, President Herbert Hoover was the first to light up the world's new tallest building. He pushed a button and the building was **illuminated**—from about 200 miles (322 km) away!

HERBERT HOOVER

Window washers, like this man in 1935, have to wear special safety gear while they're working.

A NEW JOB CAME ABOUT BECAUSE SKYSCRAPERS LIKE THE EMPIRE STATE BUILDING WERE BUILT.

The Empire State Building has 6,514 windows, and they all need to be cleaned. Window washing can be dangerous work—and cleaning one big skyscraper can take over a month!

KING KONG

THE EMPIRE STATE BUILDING WAS FEATURED IN A MOVIE IN 1933!

Only 2 years after it was finished, the Empire State Building was on the big screen in *King Kong*. In the movie, a giant ape called King Kong climbs the building, swats at planes trying to capture him, and falls to his death.

King Kong didn't climb the real Empire State Building. An 18-inch (46 cm) tall model of the ape climbed a mini Empire State Building when the movie was made.

KING KONG

FAY WRAY

THE BUILDING'S LIGHTS WERE DIMMED TO HONOR A DEATH IN 2004.

Actress Fay Wray played the woman King Kong loved in *King Kong*. The lights of the Empire State Building are rarely put out, but 2 days after Wray died, they were dimmed for 15 minutes.

DRAMATIC EVENTS

A PLANE HIT THE EMPIRE STATE BUILDING IN 1945!

Pilot William Franklin Smith Jr. believed he could successfully fly on a foggy July morning. He accidentally crashed into an upper floor of the building, killing 14 people.

Smith was flying a B-25 bomber when he crashed into the Empire State Building.

An Australian man named Paul Crake holds the record for fastest ascent. He set the record in 2003.

THE RECORD FOR FASTEST ASCENT OF THE EMPIRE STATE BUILDING IS 9 MINUTES, 33 SECONDS.

Every year, **participants** in the Empire State Building Run-Up race up 1,576 stairs to the 86th floor! People travel from all over the world to **compete**.

FUN FACT: 14

THE EMPIRE STATE BUILDING IS STRUCK BY LIGHTNING ABOUT 20 TIMES A YEAR.

Don't worry—no one will get hurt! There's a **lightning rod** at the top of the building so the lightning strikes don't cause damage or injury.

MORE THAN 30 PEOPLE HAVE JUMPED OFF THE EMPIRE STATE BUILDING.

Daredevil Thor Alex Kappfjell successfully jumped off the Empire State Building in 1998. He was arrested for jumping off the World Trade Center 6 months later.

Some of those who have jumped died. However, some people still try to jump off the building for fun using special gear! This isn't allowed and those who try it can be arrested by the police.

VISITING THE EMPIRE STATE BUILDING

FUN FACT: 16

NO OTHER BUILDING IN NEW YORK SHARES THE EMPIRE STATE BUILDING'S ZIP CODE.

The building is found in the 10001 zip code of Manhattan. However, in 1980, the building was given the zip code 10118. It's because there are so many businesses there.

EMPIRE STATE BUILDING

MANHATTAN, NEW YORK

You have to pay to go up
to the observation decks, but
anyone can walk into the
lobby for free!

EMPIRE STATE

INFORMATION

FUN FACT: 17

ABOUT 4 MILLION PEOPLE VISIT THE EMPIRE STATE
BUILDING EVERY YEAR.

Visitors can visit the observation decks, learn about the

building, and even enjoy a meal at one of the restaurants

located throughout the building.

THE HIGHEST OBSERVATION DECK CAN ONLY BE REACHED BY A **MANUALLY** OPERATED ELEVATOR.

The other elevators in the building have been updated over the years, but not this one! Many visitors come to ride in this special elevator that only goes to the "Top Deck." This observation deck is found on the 102nd floor.

TOP DECK

The main observation deck is found on the 86th floor.

The views from the top deck of the Empire State Building are some of the best in New York City!

ON A CLEAR DAY, YOU CAN SEE FIVE STATES FROM THE TOP DECK.

New York, New Jersey, Massachusetts, Pennsylvania, and Connecticut can be seen from this high point. In fact, visitors can see a distance of about 80 miles (129 km) in all directions!

THERE'S A "SECRET" 103RD FLOOR OF THE EMPIRE STATE BUILDING.

Most visitors can only get as high as the 102nd floor, but if you're a celebrity, politician, or other important person, you may be able to get a special invitation to the private observatory on the 103rd floor!

New York Mets player Jason Bay is one of the lucky few to have visited the 103rd floor!

EMPIRE STATE BUILDING TIMELINE

MARCH 17, 1930
CONSTRUCTION BEGINS.

APRIL 1931
THE BUILDING IS FINISHED.

MAY 1, 1931
PRESIDENT HERBERT HOOVER TURNS ON THE BUILDING'S LIGHTS BY PRESSING A BUTTON IN WASHINGTON, DC. THIS IS THE OFFICIAL OPENING OF THE BUILDING.

JULY 28, 1945
A PLANE CRASHES INTO THE BUILDING, KILLING 14 PEOPLE.

1971
THE NORTH TOWER OF THE WORLD TRADE CENTER TAKES OVER AS THE TALLEST BUILDING IN THE WORLD.

MAY 18, 1981
THE EMPIRE STATE BUILDING IS DECLARED A LANDMARK.

SEPTEMBER 11, 2001
THE WORLD TRADE CENTER FALLS, AND THE EMPIRE STATE BUILDING IS ONCE AGAIN THE TALLEST BUILDING IN NEW YORK CITY.

APRIL 30, 2012
ONE WORLD TRADE CENTER IS COMPLETED, AND IT'S TALLER THAN THE EMPIRE STATE BUILDING.

A GLOBAL ICON

The Empire State Building has been one of Americans' favorite buildings since its construction in 1931. Its beauty and height make it recognizable to everyone who visits New York City. It stands as a symbol of hope and the ability to achieve the impossible.

The Empire State Building will continue to be visited and admired by people all over the world for years to come, especially as it's updated to meet the needs of the 21st century visitor!

At night, visitors can see the LED tower lights installed in 2012.

GLOSSARY

antenna: a metal rod or wire used to send and receive radio waves

ascent: the act of climbing up something

compete: to try to win a contest with others

illuminate: to light up

labor: to do work

lightning rod: a metal rod placed at the top of a building to safely direct lightning into the ground

manual: operated or controlled with the hands or by a person

participant: someone who takes part in something

skyscraper: a very tall building in a city

zip code: a group of numbers that is used in the United States as part of an address to identify a mail delivery area

FOR MORE INFORMATION

BOOKS

Lassieur, Alison. *Building the Empire State Building: An Interactive Engineering Adventure.* North Mankato, MN: Capstone Press, 2015.

Pascal, Janet B. *Where Is the Empire State Building?* New York, NY: Grosset & Dunlap, 2015.

WEBSITES

Building the Empire State Building: The Daredevil Sky Boys
www.walksofnewyork.com/blog/how-was-the-empire-state-building-built
The sky boys' story comes to life on this informative website.

10 Surprising Facts About the Empire State Building
www.history.com/news/10-surprising-facts-about-the-empire-state-building
Find interesting pictures and facts about the Empire State Building here.

US History: Empire State Building
www.ducksters.com/history/us_1900s/empire_state_building.php
This site offers information about the Empire State Building in an easy-to-understand format for kids.

Publisher's note to educators and parents: Our editors have carefully reviewed these websites to ensure that they are suitable for students. Many websites change frequently, however, and we cannot guarantee that a site's future contents will continue to meet our high standards of quality and educational value. Be advised that students should be closely supervised whenever they access the internet.

INDEX